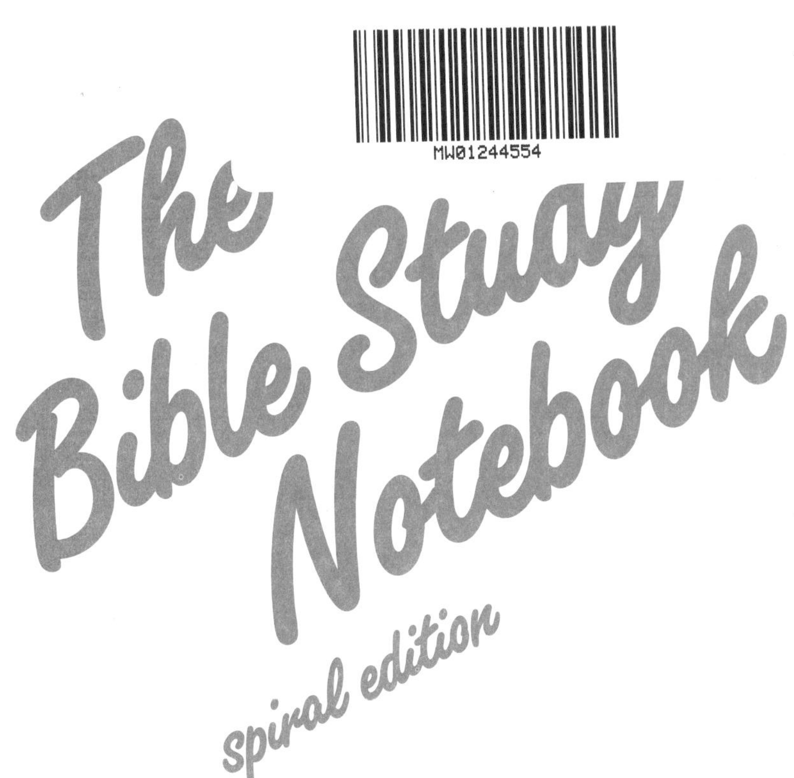
MW01244554
The
Bible Study
Notebook
spiral edition

MERIDIAN
PUBLICATIONS

Revised and reprinted in 1996 by Meridian, 3040 Charlevoix Dr. SE,
Grand Rapids, Michigan 49546-7091

Over 250,000 sold this edition.

Cover design by Robert S. Alderink and David M. Versluis
Book design by Robert S. Alterink and David M. Versluis

M0252 Spiral Edition 1-56570-025-2

Manufactured in the United States of America

MERIDIAN
PUBLICATIONS

Scripture Chapter & Verse Reference

BOOK OF BIBLE/TOPIC

SPEAKER/TEACHER

DATE

TITLE

SCRIPTURE

THEME/INTRODUCTION

OUTLINE & ILLUSTRATIONS

Outline & Illustration continued

Scriptu
Chapte
Verse
Referer

Application: Things To Do

ripture
apter &
Verse
ference

BOOK OF BIBLE/TOPIC

SPEAKER/TEACHER

DATE

TITLE

SCRIPTURE

THEME/INTRODUCTION

OUTLINE & ILLUSTRATIONS

Outline & Illustration continued

Scripture
Chapter
Verse
Reference

Application: Things To Do

ripture
apter &
Verse
erence

BOOK OF BIBLE/TOPIC

SPEAKER/TEACHER

DATE

TITLE

SCRIPTURE

THEME/INTRODUCTION

OUTLINE & ILLUSTRATIONS

Outline & Illustration continued

Scriptu
Chapte
Verse
Referen

Application: Things To Do

cripture
apter &
Verse
eference

BOOK OF BIBLE/TOPIC

SPEAKER/TEACHER

DATE

TITLE

SCRIPTURE

THEME/INTRODUCTION

OUTLINE & ILLUSTRATIONS

Scriptu
Chapter
Verse
Referen

Application: Things To Do

cripture
apter &
Verse
ference

BOOK OF BIBLE/TOPIC

SPEAKER/TEACHER

DATE

TITLE

SCRIPTURE

THEME/INTRODUCTION

OUTLINE & ILLUSTRATIONS

Outline & Illustration continued

Scriptu
Chapte
Verse
Referer

Application: Things To Do

cripture
apter &
Verse
eference

Book of Bible/Topic

Speaker/Teacher

Date

Title

Scripture

Theme/Introduction

Outline & Illustrations

Outline & Illustration continued

Scriptur
Chapter
Verse
Referen

Application: Things To Do

cripture
apter &
Verse
eference

BOOK OF BIBLE/TOPIC

SPEAKER/TEACHER

DATE

TITLE

SCRIPTURE

THEME/INTRODUCTION

OUTLINE & ILLUSTRATIONS

Scripture Chapter Verse Reference

Outline & Illustration continued

Application: Things To Do

cripture
napter &
Verse
eference

BOOK OF BIBLE/TOPIC

SPEAKER/TEACHER

DATE

TITLE

SCRIPTURE

THEME/INTRODUCTION

OUTLINE & ILLUSTRATIONS

Outline & Illustration continued

Scripture
Chapter
Verse
Reference

Application: Things To Do

cripture
apter &
Verse
eference

BOOK OF BIBLE/TOPIC

SPEAKER/TEACHER

DATE

TITLE

SCRIPTURE

THEME/INTRODUCTION

OUTLINE & ILLUSTRATIONS

Outline & Illustration continued

Scripture
Chapter
Verse
Reference

Application: Things To Do

Scripture
Chapter &
Verse
Reference

BOOK OF BIBLE/TOPIC

SPEAKER/TEACHER

DATE

TITLE

SCRIPTURE

THEME/INTRODUCTION

OUTLINE & ILLUSTRATIONS

Outline & Illustration continued

Scripture
Chapter
Verse
Reference

Application: Things To Do

Scripture Chapter & Verse Reference

BOOK OF BIBLE/TOPIC

SPEAKER/TEACHER

DATE

TITLE

SCRIPTURE

THEME/INTRODUCTION

OUTLINE & ILLUSTRATIONS

Outline & Illustration continued

Scriptur
Chapter
Verse
Referen

Application: Things To Do

cripture
apter &
Verse
eference

BOOK OF BIBLE/TOPIC

SPEAKER/TEACHER

DATE

TITLE

SCRIPTURE

THEME/INTRODUCTION

OUTLINE & ILLUSTRATIONS

Outline & Illustration continued

Scriptu
Chapter
Verse
Referen

Application: Things To Do

cripture
apter &
Verse
eference

BOOK OF BIBLE/TOPIC

SPEAKER/TEACHER

DATE

TITLE

SCRIPTURE

THEME/INTRODUCTION

OUTLINE & ILLUSTRATIONS

Outline & Illustration continued

Scriptu
Chapter
Verse
Referen

Application: Things To Do

cripture
apter &
Verse
ference

BOOK OF BIBLE/TOPIC

SPEAKER/TEACHER

DATE

TITLE

SCRIPTURE

THEME/INTRODUCTION

OUTLINE & ILLUSTRATIONS

Outline & Illustration continued

Scriptu
Chapte
Verse
Referer

Application: Things To Do

ripture
apter &
Verse
ference

BOOK OF BIBLE/TOPIC

SPEAKER/TEACHER

DATE

TITLE

SCRIPTURE

THEME/INTRODUCTION

OUTLINE & ILLUSTRATIONS

Outline & Illustration continued

Script
Chapt
Verse
Refere

Application: Things To Do

ripture
pter &
Verse
erence

BOOK OF BIBLE/TOPIC

SPEAKER/TEACHER

DATE

TITLE

SCRIPTURE

THEME/INTRODUCTION

OUTLINE & ILLUSTRATIONS

Outline & Illustration continued

Script
Chapt
Verse
Refere

Application: Things To Do

ripture
apter &
Verse
ference

BOOK OF BIBLE/TOPIC

SPEAKER/TEACHER

DATE

TITLE

SCRIPTURE

THEME/INTRODUCTION

OUTLINE & ILLUSTRATIONS

Outline & Illustration continued

Script
Chapt
Verse
Refere

Application: Things To Do

cripture
apter &
Verse
ference

BOOK OF BIBLE/TOPIC

SPEAKER/TEACHER

DATE

TITLE

SCRIPTURE

THEME/INTRODUCTION

OUTLINE & ILLUSTRATIONS

Outline & Illustration continued

Scripture
Chapter
Verse
Reference

Application: Things To Do

ripture
pter &
Verse
erence

BOOK OF BIBLE/TOPIC

SPEAKER/TEACHER

DATE

TITLE

SCRIPTURE

THEME/INTRODUCTION

OUTLINE & ILLUSTRATIONS

Outline & Illustration continued

Scriptu
Chapte
Verse
Referen

Application: Things To Do

ripture
pter &
Verse
erence

Book of Bible/Topic

Speaker/Teacher

Date

Title

Scripture

Theme/Introduction

Outline & Illustrations

Outline & Illustration continued

Scriptu
Chapte
Verse
Referer

Application: Things To Do

ipture
pter &
Verse
erence

BOOK OF BIBLE/TOPIC

SPEAKER/TEACHER

DATE

TITLE

SCRIPTURE

THEME/INTRODUCTION

OUTLINE & ILLUSTRATIONS

Outline & Illustration continued

Scriptu
Chapte
Verse
Refere

Application: Things To Do

ipture
pter &
Verse
erence

BOOK OF BIBLE/TOPIC

SPEAKER/TEACHER

DATE

TITLE

SCRIPTURE

THEME/INTRODUCTION

OUTLINE & ILLUSTRATIONS

Outline & Illustration continued

Scriptu
Chapte
Verse
Refere

Application: Things To Do

ripture
pter &
Verse
erence

BOOK OF BIBLE/TOPIC

SPEAKER/TEACHER

DATE

TITLE

SCRIPTURE

THEME/INTRODUCTION

OUTLINE & ILLUSTRATIONS

Outline & Illustration continued

Scriptu
Chapter
Verse
Referen

Application: Things To Do

ripture
apter &
Verse
erence

Book of Bible/Topic

Speaker/Teacher

Date

Title

Scripture

Theme/Introduction

Outline & Illustrations

Outline & Illustration continued

Scriptu
Chapte
Verse
Referen

Application: Things To Do

ripture
pter &
Verse
erence

Book of Bible/Topic

Speaker/Teacher

Date

Title

Scripture

Theme/Introduction

Outline & Illustrations

Outline & Illustration continued

Scriptu
Chapter
Verse
Referen

Application: Things To Do

ripture
pter &
Verse
erence

BOOK OF BIBLE/TOPIC

SPEAKER/TEACHER

DATE

TITLE

SCRIPTURE

THEME/INTRODUCTION

OUTLINE & ILLUSTRATIONS

Outline & Illustration continued

Scriptu
Chapte
Verse
Referer

Application: Things To Do

cripture
apter &
Verse
ference

BOOK OF BIBLE/TOPIC

SPEAKER/TEACHER

DATE

TITLE

SCRIPTURE

THEME/INTRODUCTION

OUTLINE & ILLUSTRATIONS

OUTLINE & ILLUSTRATION continued

Script
Chapte
Verse
Refere

APPLICATION: THINGS TO DO

cripture
apter &
Verse
ference

BOOK OF BIBLE/TOPIC

SPEAKER/TEACHER

DATE

TITLE

SCRIPTURE

THEME/INTRODUCTION

OUTLINE & ILLUSTRATIONS

Outline & Illustration continued

Scripture
Chapter
Verse
Reference

Application: Things To Do

cripture
apter &
Verse
ference

BOOK OF BIBLE/TOPIC

SPEAKER/TEACHER

DATE

TITLE

SCRIPTURE

THEME/INTRODUCTION

OUTLINE & ILLUSTRATIONS

Outline & Illustration continued

Script
Chapte
Verse
Refere

Application: Things To Do

ripture
pter &
Verse
erence

BOOK OF BIBLE/TOPIC

SPEAKER/TEACHER

DATE

TITLE

SCRIPTURE

THEME/INTRODUCTION

OUTLINE & ILLUSTRATIONS

Outline & Illustration continued

Script
Chapt
Verse
Refere

Application: Things To Do